CITIES OF THE WORLD

ST. PETERSBURG

BY DEBORAH KENT

CHILDREN'S PRESS®
A Division of Grolier Publishing
New York London Hong Kong Sydney
Danbury, Connecticut

CONSULTANTS

Ilya Kutik, Ph.D.
Assistant Professor
Department of Slavic Languages and Literature
Northwestern University

Linda Cornwell
Learning Resource Consultant
Indiana Department of Education

Project Editor: Downing Publishing Services
Design Director: Karen Kohn & Associates, Ltd.
Photo Researcher: Jan Izzo
Pronunciations: Courtesy of Laura Shear, Ph.D. candidate, Russian Language and Literature, University of Chicago, and Tony Breed, M.A., Linguistics, Universitiy of Chicago

---

NOTES ON RUSSIAN PRONUNCIATION

Most of the pronunciations in this book are exactly as they look, with the following notes: *ah* is like *a* in father; *ar* is as in far; *aw* is as in draw; *oo* is as in food; *igh* is as in light; *ts* is always as in gets; *j* is as in jar; *zh* is like the *s* in pleasure. Some sounds in Russian do not occur in English: *uy* is a vowel that sounds something like the *ih* sound in bit; <u>h</u> is like the *h* in hat but stronger and harsher. If you try to say *k* as in kite but relax and slur the sound, it will sound like <u>h</u>.

Library of Congress Cataloging-in-Publication Data
Kent, Deborah.
      St. Petersburg / by Deborah Kent.
       p.   cm. — (Cities of the world)
      Includes bibliographical references and index.
      Summary: Describes the history, culture, daily life, food, people, and points of interest of Russia's second-largest city.
      ISBN 0-516-20467-X
      1. Saint Petersburg (Russia) — Juvenile literature.   [l. Saint Petersburg (Russia)]
   I. Title.   II. Series: Cities of the world (New York, N.Y.)
DK552.K46   1997   97-6161
947'. 21—dc21   CIP
                                               AC

TABLE OF CONTENTS

EMPERORS

On a clear summer day, people throng St. Petersburg's Palace Square. The square is a vast, open space where people gather for rallies and ceremonies. The square is best known for the magnificent buildings around it. The chance to admire these historic structures lures crowds to the square.

On the edge of the square stands the Winter Palace, one of the most extraordinary buildings in all of Russia. The palace is immense, longer than two football fields. It bristles with ornate turrets and balconies. The Winter Palace is a relic of the era when St. Petersburg was the imperial capital of the Russian Empire.

For more than 150 years, the Winter Palace was home to Russia's emperors, or *tsars*. They filled its halls with priceless paintings.

Below: The Golden Room at the Hermitage

Above and opposite page: The Winter Palace on Palace Square is now known as the Hermitage Museum.

tsar (TSAHR)

Nobles wandered the palace's luxurious gardens, adorned with statues and splashing fountains. The palace was strictly off limits for the common people.

In the twentieth century, Palace Square witnessed enormous changes. It saw the fall of the tsars and the rise of a Communist government. It watched Communism crumble into ruins. The square has been the scene of angry protests as the Russian people struggle to build a new society.

Today, the gates of the Winter Palace stand open to all the people of Russia. The tsars are gone, and their royal treasures are on display for the world to see. Now known as the Hermitage Museum, the Winter Palace belongs to everyone.

As they gaze up at the Winter Palace, the people of St. Petersburg marvel at the richness of their heritage. St. Petersburg is a thriving seaport and a bustling factory town. It is a lively cultural center and a showcase of art and architecture. Through all of its changes, St. Petersburg remains one of the world's great cities.

St. Petersburg lies in the far north. It has the same latitude as Anchorage, Alaska. Winter days are short in St. Petersburg. The sun rises at nine in the morning and sets at four in the afternoon. People hurry along the streets, bundled in shawls and furs. Many wear hats with heavy flaps to protect their ears from frostbite.

Then, at last, the long, bleak winter is over. Spring smiles on St. Petersburg once more. In June, people crowd the parks and beaches. For about three weeks, the sun never goes down. It bathes the city in a soft, warm glow all night long. These "white nights" are nature's gift to St. Petersburg. They remind the people that another ordeal is behind them. Once again, they are survivors.

THE CITY ON THE NEVA

With nearly 5 million people, St. Petersburg is the second largest city in Russia. Only Moscow, the capital, is bigger. St. Petersburg lies on the eastern end of the Gulf of Finland, an arm of the Baltic Sea. To the north sprawls Lake Ladoga. The city stands on 42 islands at the marshy delta of the Neva River. The islands are separated by the Neva's many winding branches. The city is also crisscrossed by a network of canals. These canals link the river's tributaries to one another.

Ladoga (LAH-DUH-GUH)
Neva (NYEE-VAH)
Nevsky Prospekt (NYEHV-skee prahss-PYEKT)

Above: A boat on one of St. Petersburg's many canals
Left: A Russian naval cap
Below: Russian navy recruits
Opposite page: The Neva River with the Peter and Paul Fortress in the background and a sailing ship in the foreground

The people of St. Petersburg are never far from water, whether it is a canal, a river, or the sea itself. Sailing and ship-building have played a major role in the city's history. St. Petersburg is Russia's busiest seaport. Huge cargo ships load and unload along its wharves.

Smaller boats glide up and down the Neva and along the canals.

On a map, the streets of St. Petersburg form a clear, gridlike pattern. They are straight and broad, perfect for holding parades. The main thoroughfare is called the Nevsky Prospekt. The

Nevsky Prospekt is lined with monuments and magnificent stone buildings. It leads through the center of the city to the Peter and Paul Fortress on the Gulf of Finland. The city grew up around this imposing structure, which was built early in the eighteenth century. The

fortress makes the city's name especially fitting. Peter comes from a Greek word meaning "rock." Burg is a German word for "fortress." St. Petersburg is the city of the stone fortress. In fact, it has so many splendid stone buildings that it is often called the "City of Stone."

THE PEOPLE OF ST. PETERSBURG

As they pass a church, St. Petersburgers sometimes make the sign of the cross. They tend to make the gesture a little awkwardly and self-consciously. It does not come naturally yet, but they are trying to learn.

Some of the most spectacular buildings in St. Petersburg are houses of worship. But for 75 years, from 1917 until 1991, Russia's Communist government discouraged religious practices throughout the nation. Few people in St. Petersburg attended church services. Holidays such as Christmas and Easter were nearly forgotten. Most churches were turned into museums.

Left: The colorful and ornate onion domes of the Church of the Resurrection
Above: A funeral service at Preobrojensky Russian Orthodox Church

Russia's Communist government collapsed in 1991. The breakdown of the Communist system brought radical changes to St. Petersburg. Many people looked to the past for answers to troubling questions. They began returning to the churches where their grandparents and great-grandparents worshiped nearly a century before.

St. Petersburg has several Protestant churches, Jewish synagogues, and a Buddhist temple. The majority of the city's churchgoers belong to the Eastern Orthodox faith. Eastern Christians broke away from the Western (or Roman Catholic) Church in A.D. 1054. Russian

Orthodox churches are richly decorated with religious art. January 7, Russian Christmas, is now an official holiday.

Eggs decorated for Easter in the Russian tradition

Dating Troubles

Why does Russia celebrate Christmas on January 7 instead of December 25? The answer goes back to 1582. In that year, much of Europe switched to a new calendar designed by Roman Catholic Pope Gregory XIII. Christmas fell on December 25 according to this new "Gregorian Calendar." Russia kept the earlier "Julian Calendar," by which Christmas fell in January. The Julian Calendar is still used by the Russian Orthodox Church. However, the Russian government changed to the Gregorian Calendar in 1918. The revolution of October 1917 took place while the old Julian Calendar was still in effect. As a result, Russians today celebrate the anniversary of the October Revolution in November.

Left: Two young Russian girls from the folk group called Divo

Below: The book cover of a classic Russian fairy tale

Most St. Petersburgers speak the Russian language and consider themselves to be of pure Russian heritage. However, people of many minority groups also live in the city. Among them are Ukrainians and Turkmenians. These groups have unique languages and traditions. Turkmenia and the Ukraine were states within the Union of Soviet Socialist Republics (USSR), which broke apart in 1991. St. Petersburg also has communities of Gypsies and Jews.

St. Petersburgers place great value on learning. The city overflows with libraries, museums, and universities. It is not expensive to attend college. College students must study very hard, however. They have little spare time for dating and going to parties.

Teens in St. Petersburg are fascinated by music and movies from western Europe and the United States. They are hungry to buy blue jeans, CDs, and videocassettes. Most of these items are very expensive in St. Petersburg stores. For years, they were seldom available at all. Even basic necessities were often hard to come by.

This group of university students in St. Petersburg is wearing clothing styles that are popular in western Europe and the United States.

Ukraine (YOO-CRANE)
Turkmenia (TOORK-MYEH-NEE-YUH)

MAKING THE BEST OF IT

During the Communist era, shopping in St. Petersburg could take all day. In order to buy milk, eggs, bread, or vegetables, people had to wait in long lines at the store. Often, the items wanted were sold out by the time most customers reached the grocery counter. Patiently, they turned away and tried another shop, where they waited in yet another line.

For 75 years, the Russian people lived under a Communist government. Communism promised to create a society in which all people would be equal to one another. No longer would some live in luxury while others were desperately poor. The government would control all businesses and divide their profits evenly among the people.

Communism sounded like a good idea at first. Sadly, however, it had many failings. It provided jobs for nearly everyone, but most people did not work as hard as they could.

Left: Two women selling plastic bags on a St. Petersburg street

They knew they would earn the same amount of money no matter what they did. Most people did not earn very much. Russians sometimes joked, "We pretend to work, and they pretend to pay us."

Getting Around

Only the richest St. Petersburgers can afford to own automobiles. Most people travel within the city by bus or subway. The subway system, known as the Metro, was completed in 1955. It is beautifully clean and efficient. It is also very crowded. St. Petersburgers are proud of their Metro. But they dream of buying cars and taking to the road.

During the Communist era, these Russians stood in a long line hoping to buy fresh strawberries.

Because Russian markets today usually have plenty of food for sale, lines are not long. Prices are high, however.

After Russia's Communist government collapsed in 1991, the people of St. Petersburg had new freedom to set up their own businesses. But the price of most goods is high, and salaries remain very low. On average, St. Petersburgers earn only $100 per month.

Some enterprising St. Petersburgers peddle goods on the streets. From carts and stands they sell shoes, glasses, candy, toys, cassettes, and cameras. Most of these items are foreign-made. They come into the country illegally on the "black market." Buying smuggled goods on the black market is an accepted part of life in St. Petersburg. Often it is the only way for people to get the things they want or need.

Russian street peddlers selling goods from a stand

Housing is also in short supply. The city is ringed by new developments that sprang up during the 1970s and 1980s. Many St. Petersburg families still live in communal, or shared, apartments. Beside the door of each communal apartment is a list of signals for visitors. The Federovs answer two long rings of the bell. For the Dichensky family, give two short rings and a long one. Three short rings will bring Mrs. Panova to the door.

Each family in a communal apartment has one or two rooms of its own. Everyone shares the kitchen and the bathroom. St. Petersburgers stand in line to make toast in the morning. They stand in line to brush their teeth at night.

St. Petersburgers meet these inconveniences with patience and good humor. They have learned to make the best of whatever fate hands them. Despite its shortcomings, they take pride in their city and its achievements.

Federov (FYOH-DUH-RUFF)
Dichensky (DEECH-YEN-SKEE)
Panova (PUH-NOH-VUH)

These Russian schoolgirls live in the Vyborg section of St. Petersburg.

Long, long ago, according to legend, a king tried to build a city at the mouth of the Neva River. All of the houses sank into the muddy ground. Again and again, kings tried to found cities on the marshy spot. But each time, the buildings were sucked out of sight. At last, a mighty Russian giant strode to the riverbank. On his shoulders he carried a city made of iron. The giant set his city down on the marsh, and it rested firmly in place.

Russian tsar Peter I (known today as Peter the Great) was much like that legendary giant. The city Peter founded was built of stone, not iron. But to this day, it stands firmly on the marshes at the mouth of the Neva.

GREAT RESULTS FROM SMALL BEGINNINGS

When Prince Peter of Russia was fifteen, he found a battered English sailboat in a stable at his Moscow palace. The old boat became Peter's special project. He spent many happy hours hammering, caulking, and painting it. At last, the boat looked better than it did when it was brand new.

As a young man, Peter visited London and Amsterdam. He was fascinated by European shipbuilding and architecture. Peter felt that western Europe was far more advanced than Russia. When he was crowned Emperor Peter I, he determined to bring European culture to his native land.

Tsar Peter I, known as Peter the Great (above), rebuilt an old English boat when he was a boy of fifteen (right).

For 700 years, Russia had been locked in a series of wars with Sweden. In 1702, Peter drove the Swedes from the marshy islands at the mouth of the Neva River. He ordered the building of a powerful fortress to keep the region in Russian hands. The emperor lived in a cabin on the marsh and super-vised construction himself. Most of the work was done by laborers called serfs. Serfs were peasants who belonged to their land-holding masters. They were slaves who could be bought and sold.

The fort that Peter built was christened the Fortress of Saints Peter and Paul. The Peter and Paul Fortress, as it is known, became the hub of a splen-did new city. Peter admired Europe so much that he gave his city a German name, St. Petersburg. He wanted St. Petersburg to be "a window into Europe."

Above: Musicians at the entrance to the Peter and Paul Fortress

As the city grew, Peter brought in a crew of European engineers and architects. They modeled St. Petersburg on the grandest cities of western Europe. They laid out straight, wide avenues and stately squares. Their churches and palaces were monuments to Peter's ambitions.

St. Petersburg had a fine harbor and promised to be a major seaport. Not far from the fortress, Peter opened a shipyard known as the Admiralty. Skilled shipwrights created a fleet of warships and merchant vessels. The harbor bristled with masts. The wharves rang with shouts as men loaded and unloaded crates, bales, and barrels. Soon, St. Petersburg was the busiest port in Russia.

These boys participated in a military parade in honor of Peter the Great.

In 1712, Peter I moved Russia's capital from Moscow to St. Petersburg. After all his achievements, he still remembered the boat he had rebuilt when he was a boy. He called it the "grandfather of the Russian fleet." In 1723, he had it hauled to St. Petersburg by cart. The emperor himself launched the little boat on the Neva. In triumph, he sailed past the forts and palaces of his shining new capital. The imperial fleet saluted him with cannons and fireworks. Across the sky, the fireworks formed flaming words, "From small beginnings may come great results."

Above: Sextants like the antique shown above may have been used for navigation by the Russian fleet in the time of Peter the Great.

Right: Shipwrights working at the Admiralty (right, as it looks today) built Peter I's fleet of warships and merchant vessels.

STEAL WHAT IS STOLEN!

For nearly two centuries, the Russian court lived in luxury at St. Petersburg. The emperors, or tsars, resided in the magnificent Winter Palace. They also built many other palaces for themselves and their supporters. The tsars and nobles filled their halls with paintings by the world's finest artists. They feasted on the greatest delicacies the land could provide. Their banquet tables were laden with veal, venison, pheasant, oysters, and creamy desserts.

While the nobles feasted, the serfs struggled and starved. Russia abolished serfdom in 1861, but most peasants went on living in poverty. Peasants streamed into St. Petersburg to work in the city's factories. They crowded tiny, run-down

Below: Russia's last imperial family; from left to right, the tsar's daughters the Grand Duchesses Olga and Maria; Tsar Nicholas II; his wife, Empress Alexandria; his daughter Grand Duchess Anastasia; his son, Grand Duke Alexis; and his daughter Grand Duchess Tatiana
Right: A traditional Russian tea glass

houses on garbage-strewn streets. There was not enough food or clean water. Many people died of hunger and disease.

Early in the twentieth century, dynamic new leaders arose among Russia's workers. They gave impassioned speeches on assembly lines, at schools, and in public squares. They described a new system of government called Communism. No longer would some be immensely rich while others starved. Under Communism, all people would be equal. The Communist revolutionaries, or Bolsheviks, told the people that they must overthrow the tsars. They must steal back everything the tsars had stolen from them.

Bolshevik (BOLE-SHEH-VICK)

The Man Who Wouldn't Die

Tsar Nicholas II and his wife believed that Grigory Rasputin (1872–1916) was a holy man with healing powers. He seemed to have the ability to ease the suffering of their young son, who was chronically ill. Rasputin gained tremendous influence at the imperial court. To get rid of him, his enemies invited him to dinner and gave him an eclair laced with poison. Rasputin went on laughing and talking as if the poison had no effect on him. The conspirators then shot him, tied his hands and feet, and threw him into the Neva River. Rasputin managed to untie his bonds, but he drowned in the icy water.

Communist leader V. I. Lenin, speaking in a Petrograd square, urges the people to overthrow the provisional government of Russia.

In 1914, a devastating war swept across Europe. Russia plunged into the fighting. In a burst of patriotism, the Russians got rid of their capital's German name. St. Petersburg was re-christened Petrograd.

During the war, food supplies ran low in Petrograd. The Bolsheviks urged the desperate people to rebel. Early in 1917, Tsar Nicholas II gave up his throne. A provisional government tried to keep the Communists from seizing control. The new government moved into the Winter Palace, once home of the tsars.

Petrograd was in chaos. "People are stealing in a wonderfully artistic manner," wrote novelist Maxim Gorky. "Cannons, rifles, and quartermasters' supplies are being sold. The palaces of grand princes are being stolen. Everything plunderable is being plundered. Everything sellable is being sold."

In April 1917, a brilliant Communist leader named V. I. Lenin arrived in Petrograd. Lenin set to work organizing forces to overthrow the provisional government. He promised "peace to the people, land to the peasants, factories to the workers." The people rallied to Lenin's call to arms.

In October 1917, several units of the Russian navy joined Lenin's cause. The battleship *Aurora* bombarded the Winter Palace. The palace was stormed by sailors and soldiers, and the provisional government fell. Lenin installed a new Communist government at the Smolny Institute, formerly a boarding school for girls. The Communist government was headed by Lenin himself.

The Communists hailed a dazzling new era of justice and opportunity. First, however, all traces of the old imperial system had to be washed away. In the years after the revolution, thousands of people were put to death as "enemies of the state."

In 1924, after Lenin died, Petrograd received another new name. In honor of the leader of the 1917 revolution, the city was renamed Leningrad.

In July 1917, provisional government forces broke up this demonstration by workers and peasants.

Petrograd (PYEE-TROH-GRAHT)
Maxim Gorky (MUX-EEM GORE-kee)
Lenin (LYEH-NEEN)
Smolny (SMOLE-NEE)
Leningrad (LYEE-NEEN-GRAHT)

HERO CITY

"Granny died on the 25th of January. Uncle Alyosha on the 10th of May. Mummy on the 13th of May at 7:30 A.M. Everyone's dead. Only Tanya is left." In the spring of 1942, a ten-year-old Leningrad girl named Tanya Savicheva wrote these heart-wrenching lines in her diary. Russia was at war again. Leningrad was surrounded by German tanks and artillery. The Germans cut off the city's supplies of food and fuel. The people were left to suffer and die.

Germany invaded the Soviet Union in 1941, two years after World War II broke out in Europe. The terrible siege of Leningrad began on September 8, 1941, and lasted for nearly three years. During the first winter, temperatures plunged to minus 40 degrees Fahrenheit (4.4 degrees Celsius). People burned books, chairs, and tables to gain a few hours of precious warmth. But when the fires burned out, the cold always closed in again. One Leningrad

This starving Leningrad man holds his tiny bread ration during the siege of Leningrad by the German army during World War II.

Alyosha (AH-LYOH-SHUH)
Tanya Savicheva (TAHN-YUH SUH-VEECH-YEH-VUH)

boy wrote, "There used to be a stove on which we cooked omelets and sausages and soup. Mother used to sit at the table and work far into the night by the light of a lamp. . . . The flat's empty now and completely silent. It seems to have frozen and turned into an icicle, and it will only melt in the spring."

The cold ended with springtime, but the hunger went on all year round. First, cats and dogs disappeared from the streets. Then people boiled belts and shoes to make "leather soup." Some people resorted to eating the flesh of those who died of hunger. Leningraders claimed they could recognize the cannibals at a glance. They were the only people in the city with healthy pink cheeks.

This Leningrad building was in ruins after a German bomb attack during the winter of 1941–1942.

In January 1943, Russian supply trucks finally reached Leningrad across frozen Lake Ladoga. Even so, the siege dragged on for another year. Thousands of Leningraders were killed by bombs and artillery shells. Some 600,000 died of hunger and cold. In all, nearly 1 million people lost their lives. Yet, somehow, Russian forces managed to defend the city. Throughout the siege, German soldiers never set foot on Leningrad's streets.

After Germany's defeat, the world applauded the steadfast courage of Leningrad's people. Leningrad earned a new nickname, "Hero City."

When the war was over, Leningraders set to work rebuilding their city. They restored schools and apartment buildings shattered by bombs. They reconstructed bombed-out palaces in the suburbs of Pushkin and Petrodvorets (now known as Peterhof). In ten years, Leningrad's factories had become more productive than they had been before the war. Once more, Leningrad was a vital cultural center, the nation's window into Europe.

The Commumist revolution of 1917 failed to fulfill its promises. The people of Leningrad celebrated when the Communist government toppled in 1991. Almost at once, they decided to change the city's name to St. Petersburg once more. It was as though they hoped to erase all the sorrows of the past.

One of the monuments to the heroes of the siege of Leningrad

The history of St. Petersburg is weighted with overwhelming hardships. Yet the city is famous for its art, music, and dance. No matter what happens, St. Petersburgers find ways to enjoy the richness of life.

Russian coins such as these replaced those used before the fall of Communism in 1991.

The Peter and Paul Fortress as seen from the Neva River at sunset

Pushkin (POOSH-keen)
Petrodvorets (pyee-trudd-var-YETS)
Peterhof (PEE-tur-hoff)

MOMENTS

The Mouse King is fierce and menacing. His razor-sharp teeth will chew the wooden nutcracker to sawdust. But young Clara rushes to defend the nutcracker, driving the Mouse King away. Suddenly, the nutcracker springs to life. It becomes a handsome prince who leads Clara into a dream kingdom of Chinese dancers and sugarplum fairies.

Around the world each Christmastime, this familiar tale comes to life in performances of *The Nutcracker*. Composed by St. Petersburger Peter Ilich Tchaikovsky in 1892, *The Nutcracker* is the world's best-loved ballet. St. Petersburgers love dance and music, literature, theater, and art. They also enjoy sports, games, and the outdoors.

PLEASURES OF THE SEASONS

Winter in St. Petersburg is brutally cold. While storms rage outside, families and friends gather in snug kitchens. Someone may strum a guitar. Children listen as the grown-ups tell stories over glasses of fiery vodka.

St. Petersburgers do not spend the whole winter shut up at home. Sometimes, they bundle up in coats and scarves to enjoy the weather. They whoosh down snowy slopes on sleds and skis. They put on skates and race over frozen streams and canals.

Children pelt one another with snowballs and dodge behind the walls of snow fortresses.

Russian vodka glasses

Left: A St. Petersburg child enjoys sledding on a snowy winter afternoon.
Below: Many St. Petersburgers spend summer afternoons boating on the Neva River.

These girls and their parents are spending a sunny summer afternoon in a St. Petersburg park.

By the end of April, the ice breaks up on the Neva. Once again, boats can sail St. Petersburg's waterways. A few wealthy families own expensive yachts. The average family can at least rent a sailboat or a power launch for a special outing. On pleasant days, small boats crowd the river and the city's many canals.

Along the Gulf of Finland north of St. Petersburg lie sandy beaches fringed by pine forests. This area has been a resort since the days of the tsars. Today, some families still have summer homes, or *dachas*, where they can escape the bustle of the city. Many St. Petersburg children attend summer camps nestled in these quiet woods.

St. Petersburgers love sports and games of all kinds. The city has 36 stadiums. The largest of these is the Kirov Stadium. Soccer and hockey are the city's most popular team sports. Factories, neighborhoods, and schools sponsor teams that compete regularly. Many St. Petersburgers take part in swimming, diving, and gymnastics competitions.

dacha (DAH-chuh)
Kirov (KEE-ruff)

THE PERFORMING ARTS

Every evening, St. Petersburgers switch on their televisions to watch *600 Seconds*. This popular talk show deals with such issues as crime, drugs, and homelessness. Under Russia's Communist government, such topics could not be discussed in the media. Since 1991, St. Petersburgers have enjoyed a new openness. This openness is reflected in their music, theater, and film.

Rock music was frowned on by the Communists. Today, however, St. Petersburg teens collect rock cassettes and CDs. Russian and foreign rock groups perform in the parks or in indoor stadiums.

Rock music has gained a solid footing in St. Petersburg. But St. Petersburgers have not forgotten the classics. The most talented music students in Russia long to attend St. Petersburg Conservatory. Its graduates include some of the world's greatest composers. Among them are Tchaikovsky, Dmitri Shostakovich, and Igor Stravinsky.

Musicians practicing for a concert

Tchaikovsky (CHIGH-KOFF-SKEE)
Dmitri Shostakovich (DIH-MEE-TREE SHUH-STAH-KOVE-EECH)
Igor Stravinsky (EE-GUR STRUH-VEEN-SKEE)
matryoshka (muh-TRYOH-shkuh)

Surprises within Surprises

A favorite toy for Russian children is the *matryoshka*. The matryoshka is a brightly painted wooden doll that is hollow and comes apart in the middle. When you open it up, you will find a smaller doll inside. Open that to discover yet another, still smaller, doll. A matryoshka may have a dozen dolls hidden within it, the smallest barely more than a painted splinter.

The St. Petersburg Philharmonic Orchestra plays in the conservatory's concert hall. The conservatory also welcomes outstanding guest performers and conductors from all over the world.

A Russian rock band performing at St. Petersburg's Art Bar

Left: Ballet shoes
Below: A performer at the Maryinsky Theater of Ballet

St. Petersburg's ballet tradition reaches back to 1738, when the city's first school of ballet was founded. Today, tickets to performances at the Maryinsky Theater of Ballet are sold out months in advance. The Maryinsky is the most famous theater in the city. It is built to resemble an imperial palace.

Americans sometimes think that ballet is for sissies. Actually, Russian ballet dancers are as strong and supple as athletes. They bend, leap, and lift one another with such grace that their movements look effortless.

Theater came to St. Petersburg in 1746 with the founding of the Theater of Comedies and Tragedies. Today, the city has nearly 30 theaters. The Bolshoi Drama Theater and the Maly Theater put on new plays and works that have stood the test of time. Sometimes, young playwrights have their works performed in cabarets and basements. Filmmakers, too, are very active in the city. With low budgets and high energy, they create films about topics that were long forbidden.

Before 1991, the government supported theater and cinema generously, as long as they carried a pro-Communist message. The change in government has created opportunities for artistic expression. But it also brought a new set of problems. Now, St. Petersburgers can say what they like, but government funding is scarce. Playwrights, filmmakers, and artists have to scramble for money to carry out their work.

Above: Students at the Imperial Academy of Art

Maryinski (MAH-REE-YEEN-SKEE)
Bolshoi (BALL-SHOY)
Maly (MAH-LUY)

BEAUTY AND GRANDEUR

In 1764, Russian empress Catherine II, now known as Catherine the Great, began to gather works of art from all over Europe. She filled the Winter Palace with paintings and sculptures by the finest artists the world had ever known. The collection was for her private enjoyment. In a letter, Catherine wrote, "Although I am all alone, I have a whole labyrinth of rooms, and all of them are filled with luxuries. . . . Only the palace mice and myself feast our eyes on them."

Over the years, other emperors expanded the collection of art that Catherine began. Paintings and sculptures overflowed the palace and were housed in an adjoining complex of buildings called the

Catherine the Great filled the Winter Palace (left) with works of art collected from all over Europe.

Hermitage. After 1852, the Hermitage was opened to the public. Today, it is one of the most outstanding art museums on earth.

Exhibits in the Hermitage trace the art of humankind from the Stone Age to modern times. Each year, 3 million visitors walk its marble halls. They gaze at Egyptian scarab bracelets, statues of Greek gods, ivory figurines from India, and religious paintings from sixteenth-century Italy. A visitor would have to spend eight hours a day for 70 years just to glance at each piece of art in the Hermitage collection.

A pair of carved lions guards the entrance to the Russian Museum in Mikhailovsky Palace. The ground floor is adorned with swords, shields, helmets, and suits of armor. The Russian Museum displays the work of Russian artists from the tenth century to the present. Among its most prized exhibits are several medieval icons—paintings of saints that stand more than 10 feet (3 m) tall.

You don't have to go to a museum to enjoy art in St. Petersburg. Many buildings are decorated outside with elaborate carvings. Statues stand in every park and square. Art is always on public view. It is among the many striking features that await visitors to St. Petersburg.

Left: This exhibit in the Hermitage is only a tiny sample of the fabulous works of art that fill several buildings.

Right: A golden statue at the palace and garden complex of Peterhof

Mikhailovsky (MEE-HIGH-luff-skee)

St. Petersburg is sometimes called the "Venice of the North." Like Venice, Italy, it is crisscrossed by waterways. The Neva River and its tributaries cut the city into four distinct sections, or "sides." Each section has its own special sights to see.

VASILYEVSKY ISLAND

Where the two main branches of the Neva come together lies a narrow spit of land called Vasilyevsky Island. Two great red towers loom above the water at the island's tip. They are known as the Rostral Columns, from a Latin word meaning "ship's prow." The towers are decorated with carvings of ships and sailors. Within each tower, a steep spiral staircase climbs to a gas torch that shines out from the top.

Vasilyevsky Island is the site of the Strelka, a cluster of majestic eighteenth- and nineteenth-century buildings. Among them is the former Merchants' Exchange. This ornate building now houses the Naval Museum. The Naval Museum celebrates everything to do with boats and seafaring. It is crammed with model ships, ancient maps and compasses, figureheads, flags, and ships' cannons. One of its treasures is the little boat that Peter the Great rebuilt when he was a teenager.

The Strelka and the Rostral Columns on Vasilyevsky Island

Left: Mounted butterflies like this one are displayed at the Strelka's Zoological Museum.

Below: This colossal statue stands in front of one of the Rostral Columns.

Russian Literature, also known as Pushkin House. St. Petersburg has a rich literary heritage. It has been home to some of Russia's best-known writers, including Alexander Pushkin and Fyodor Dostoyevsky. Dostoyevsky's most famous novel, *Crime and Punishment,* is set in St. Petersburg. It tells the story of a murderer who flees from justice and finally finds redemption.

In 1961, the frozen body of a mammoth was uncovered in the snowfields of Siberia. Scientists concluded that the mammoth died some 40,000 years ago. Today, its stuffed remains stand in the Zoological Museum, another building of the Strelka. The museum is packed with animal specimens. They range from mounted butterflies to stuffed penguins, alligators, and tigers. About 4,000 species are represented.

Soil samples from all over Russia may not be to everyone's taste. If nothing else, St. Petersburg's Soil Museum is unique in the world. Its maps and diagrams show how various soil types affect farming and mining.

Long ago, the foreign goods that flowed into St. Petersburg were weighed and taxed at the Customs House. Like so many buildings in the city, the Customs House has been turned into a museum. It is now the Institute of

THE PETROGRAD AND VYBORG SIDES

Every day at noon, the roar of a cannon echoes over St. Petersburg's Petrograd Side. The cannon is fired from the Peter and Paul Fortress, which dominates this section of the city. The cabin where Peter the Great lived during the fort's construction is still standing. Through the winter of 1703–1704, the emperor lived there without a stove or a fireplace.

An aerial view of the Peter and Paul Fortress, which dominates the Petrograd section of St. Petersburg

Vyborg (VEE-BORK)

Soaring high over the walls of the fortress is the spire of the Peter and Paul Cathedral. The spire reaches 402 feet (122.5 m) into the sky. It is the tallest structure in the city except for the television tower. At its tip perches the figure of an angel holding a cross. The Peter and Paul Cathedral is one of several buildings within the walls of the fortress. It is the final resting place of all but one of Russia's emperors.

During the nineteenth century, the Peter and Paul Fortress served as a prison. Many political prisoners—people who tried to rebel against the government—were locked in its dungeons. Today, the fortress houses a museum on the history of Russia.

An angel holding a cross perches at the tip of the spire of the Peter and Paul Cathedral.

АЛЕКСАНДРУ СЕРГѢЕВИЧУ

Russia's Black Poet

Alexander Pushkin (1799–1837) is considered the most important poet Russia has ever produced. Born in Moscow, he spent much of his life in St. Petersburg. One of Pushkin's great-grandfathers was a black African. The poet was very proud of his African heritage. Pushkin's most famous poem, *Eugene Onegin*, tells the tragic story of a man whose life lacks a meaningful purpose.

The battleship Aurora, illuminated at night, is moored in the Neva River below the Peter and Paul Fortress.

Moored in the river below the fortress is the battleship *Aurora*. In October 1917, the *Aurora* fired on the Winter Palace at the start of the Bolshevik Revolution. Today, the ship, too, is a museum, though it is sometimes still used as a training vessel for the Russian navy.

The Vyborg Side lies east of the Petrograd Side. It is an area of factories and apartment buildings. Its most notable landmark is the Finland Railway Station. Trains roll in and out of the station day and night, linking St. Petersburg with cities all across Russia. In front of the station stands a triumphant statue of Lenin, leader of the 1917 revolution.

Above: Trains rumbling in and out of the Finland Railway Station link St. Petersburg with cities all over Russia.

Right: The battleship Aurora is sometimes used as a training vessel for student sailors such as these.

THE ADMIRALTY SIDE

St. Petersburg's Admiralty Side extends along the southern, or "Left Bank," of the Neva. Its main boulevard is the Nevsky Prospekt, a broad, tree-lined avenue running east to west. The Nevsky Prospekt is always crowded with buses, cars, and taxis. It is lined with restaurants, theaters, and shops. Gostiny Dvor, the city's largest department store, is an enormous eighteenth-century building that measures almost half a mile (nearly 1 km) around.

Because St. Petersburg is threaded with waterways, it is a city of bridges. Here and there, bridges carry the Nevsky Prospekt across streams and canals. The Anichkov Bridge across the Fontanka Canal is decorated with sculptures of galloping horses.

At the eastern end of the Nevsky Prospekt sprawls Alexander Nevsky Square. The square and the avenue are named for a Russian general of the twelfth century.

Above: Pedestrians on busy Nevsky Prospekt

Left: Griffins on Bank Bridge, which spans one of the city's many canals

Gostiny Dvor (GAHSS-TEEN-uy DVORE)
Anichkov (AH-NEECH-kuff)
Fontanka (FAHN-TAHN-kuh)
Kazan (KUH-ZAHN)
Andrei Voronikhin (UNN-DRAY vuh-rah-NEE-hyeen)

52

Composer Peter Tchaikovsky, writer Fyodor Dostoyevsky, and several of St. Petersburg's leading architects are buried in cemeteries within the square.

The gilded dome of St. Isaac's Cathedral can be seen all over St. Petersburg. The great dome is covered with 200 pounds (91 kg) of pure gold. In 1818, French architect Auguste Montferrand began work on the cathedral. The work went on for the next 40 years. Many St. Petersburgers were convinced the cathedral would never be finished. Inside, St. Isaac's is decorated with stunning designs of semiprecious stones and elaborate religious sculptures. One detailed relief shows the Wise Men offering their gifts to the Christ Child.

The square in front of the Kazan Cathedral is a popular place for friends to meet. Since St. Petersburgers now feel free to express their opinions, it has also become a site for political demonstrations. Completed in 1811, the Kazan Cathedral was the work of Andrei Voronikhin. Born a serf, Voronikhin managed to become one of the leading architects of the land. The cathedral's grand portico is graced with 96 40-foot (12-m) columns. Following the revolution of 1917, the church was used as the Museum of Religion and Atheism. The museum closed after the fall of the Communist government.

Left: Inside the dome of St. Isaac's Cathedral

Right: A fashionable student in the square in front of Kazan Cathedral

In the middle of Senate Square stands the *Bronze Horseman*, an enormous statue of Peter the Great. The statue was created in 1782 by French sculptor Étienne Falconet. Its pedestal is carved from the "Thunder Stone," a 1,600-ton (1,451 metric-ton) granite boulder. Hundreds of serfs spent months dragging the Thunder Stone to St. Petersburg from a quarry 7 miles (11 km) away. When the pedestal was completed, an ugly chunk of leftover stone lay on the square. According to legend, a drunken peasant stepped forward and began to dig a pit beside it. After he had dug for four days, the stone quietly rolled into the pit. It lies beneath Senate Square to this day. Some say that the stone is a buried monument to the peasants of Russia.

The elegant eighteenth-century building known as the Admiralty stands near the western end of the Nevsky Prospekt. Originally built as the city's naval headquarters and shipyard, the Admiralty houses a naval college today. The building's spire is topped with a weather vane shaped like a frigate under full sail.

The Admiralty faces Palace Square, the oldest and most magnificent square in St. Petersburg. From its center rises the Alexander Column, a monument to Russia's 1812 victory over French emperor Napoleon. The column, which is 155 feet (47 m) high, is the tallest of its kind in the world.

The Bronze Horseman, *a huge statue of Peter the Great, stands in Senate Square.*

Raising the Column

In 1834, some 2,000 volunteers and a crew of 400 engineers gathered in Palace Square. In the middle of the square, the Alexander Column lay on its side like a sleeping giant. In a massive effort, the assembled crowd tied ropes to the mighty column, which weighed 700 tons (635 metric tons). By hauling on the ropes together, the people lifted the column to its chiseled pedestal. There it has remained.

No landmark in St. Petersburg draws more visitors than the vast Winter Palace. Its colonnade glistens white against a sky-blue background. Its roof is graced with carved figures. The Winter Palace is striking even from the outside. Inside, it is one of the world's marvels. Once the home of the tsars, it now houses the extraordinary Hermitage Museum. During the days of Imperial Russia, only tsars and nobles were allowed to view its treasures. Today, the Hermitage belongs to the people of Russia and the world.

Like the people of St. Petersburg, the Winter Palace has survived mighty upheavals. Yet it stands firm, facing the future with dignity and grace.

Above: The Alexander Column stands in the middle of Palace Square in front of the magnificent Winter Palace.

FAMOUS LANDMARKS

St. Isaac's Cathedral

The Ambassadors' Staircase at the Hermitage

The Hermitage
The Hermitage is one of the most extraordinary art museums on earth. It is housed in the Winter Palace. The museum's 400 exhibit halls can display only a fraction of the works in the entire collection.

Russian Museum
Opened in 1898, this museum features the art of Russia. In addition to paintings and sculpture, the museum displays jewelry, furniture, ceramics, and other crafts dating as far back as A.D. 1000.

Peter and Paul Cathedral
The graceful spire of this cathedral is one of St. Petersburg's beloved symbols. Completed in 1733, the cathedral stands within the walls of the Peter and Paul Fortress. The cathedral contains the tombs of most of the tsars of Russia, including Peter the Great. Today, it houses a museum on Russian history and space exploration.

Kirov Isles
These islands in the Gulf of Finland were once the summer resort of the Russian nobility. A palace built by Catherine the Great for her son Paul is now used as a hospital. The islands still have many luxurious homes for wealthy St. Petersburgers.

Komarov Botanical Institute
Some 3,500 species of plants from around the world are raised in the institute's greenhouses. Among them is the rare Korolov night cactus, whose spectacular flowers open after the summer sun goes down.

Central Naval Museum
In 1940, this museum opened in the former Stock Exchange on Vasilyevsky Island. The museum houses some 650,000 items related to ships and sailing. Among them are a wooden boat dating from A.D. 1000 and the English sailboat that Peter the Great rebuilt as a teenager.

The Kunstkammer
The Kunstkammer, or Academy of Science, was founded by Peter the Great. The emperor began a collection of unusual plants,

The spectacular fountains at Peterhof Palace

An interior view of the Maryinsky Theater

Right: One of the monument to the defenders of Leningrad in Victory Square

animals, and minerals, which he opened to the public. Today, it combines several museums into one. The Museum of Anthropology covers cultures from around the world. The Anatomical Museum includes specimens of plants and animals that became mutant after an accident at the Chernobyl Nuclear Power Plant.

Victory Square
Unveiled in 1975, this monument commemorates those who defended Leningrad during the 900-day siege of the city by the German army during World War II. Several groups of sculptures stand in the circular monument, and a memorial hall on the grounds has exhibits about life in the city during the siege.

Peterhof Palace
Built by Peter the Great, this splendid palace overlooks the Gulf of Finland. It stands on a terraced hillside above a series of grottoes and fountains called the Cascade. The palace was almost destroyed during World War II but has been reconstructed.

St. Isaac's Cathedral
The gilded dome of this cathedral is visible all over St. Petersburg. The cathedral was the life work of architect Auguste Montferrand. The interior is lavishly decorated with religious art.

Maryinsky Theater
This theater hosts performances of opera and ballet. The building resembles an imperial palace.

Field of Mars
This downtown square was created as a drilling ground for the tsar's troops. Today, it features a monument to the revolution of 1917. An eternal flame was lit in 1957 on the fortieth anniversary of the revolution. Eternal flames for all Russian memorials are lighted here.

FAST FACTS

POPULATION

City:	4,468,000
Metropolitan Area:	5,020,000

AREA   521 square miles (1,349 km^2)

The area of St. Petersburg includes several surrounding suburbs under the city's administration.

LOCATION   St. Petersburg is located in northwestern Russia. It stands at the mouth of the Neva River on the eastern end of the Gulf of Finland.

CLIMATE   St. Petersburg is famous for its long, bitter winters. February temperatures average 18 degrees Fahrenheit (-7.77° Celsius), and feel even colder because of the fierce winds. Snow lies on the ground approximately 132 days a year. Summers are mild and pleasant, though short. The average temperature in July is 64 degrees Fahrenheit (18° Celsius).

ECONOMY   St. Petersburg is the most important seaport in Russia. Shipbuilding remains a vital industry, as it has been since the city was founded. St. Petersburg is also a major manufacturing center. Factories produce machinery, chemicals, and textiles.

CHRONOLOGY

1323
Russians found a settlement called Oreshek at the delta of the Neva River

Late 1600s
Sweden controls the shores of the Baltic Sea, including the Neva Delta

1702
Peter I (the Great) drives the Swedes from the mouth of the Neva

1703
Peter builds the Peter and Paul Fortress, which becomes the heart of his new city, St. Petersburg

1711
Peter moves the imperial library from Moscow to St. Petersburg and opens it to the public

1712
St. Petersburg becomes the capital of Russia

1750
St. Petersburg has a population of 100,000

1738
St. Petersburg's first school of ballet opens

1746
The Russian Theater for Comedies and Tragedies opens in St. Petersburg

1763
Catherine the Great begins the collection of paintings that is now housed in the Hermitage Museum

1782
Étienne Falconet completes his statue of Peter the Great, known as *The Bronze Horseman*

1825
Rebels launch the Decembrist Uprising, an unsuccessful attempt to overthrow the tsar

Colorful autumn leaves decorate this Russian child and the statue she's leaning against.

1861
Russia's serfs are given their freedom

1905
Workers in St. Petersburg demonstrate for better conditions; 1,000 are gunned down on "Bloody Sunday"

1914
Russia enters World War I; St. Petersburg changes its name to Petrograd

1917
Petrograd has 2.5 million people; Tsar Nicholas II gives up his throne; in October, Lenin leads the Bolshevik Revolution and establishes a Communist government in Russia

1924
Petrograd changes its name to Leningrad

1941
In World War II, Germany invades Russia; Leningrad is under siege

1944
The siege of Leningrad ends after 900 days, leaving nearly 1 million Leningraders dead

1955
Leningrad opens its subway system, the Metro

1985
Major restoration begins at the Hermitage

1991
The Communist government in Moscow collapses; the Union of Soviet Socialist Republics breaks into several separate nations; Leningrad resumes the name St. Petersburg

ST. PETERSBURG

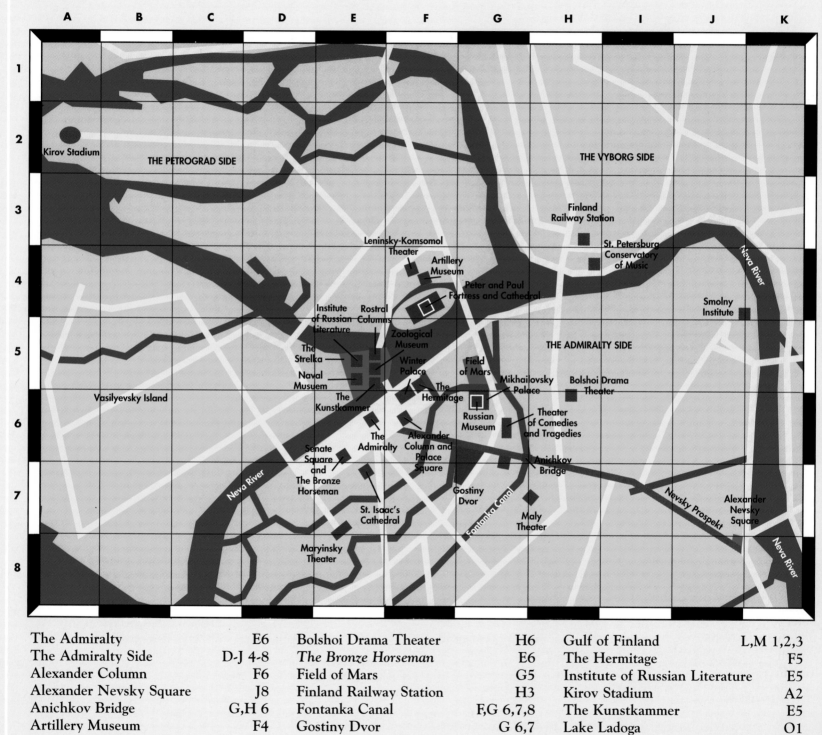

A B C D E F G H I J K

1

2
Kirov Stadium
THE PETROGRAD SIDE
THE VYBORG SIDE

3
Finland Railway Station
St. Petersburg Conservatory of Music

4
Leninsky-Komsomol Theater
Artillery Museum
Peter and Paul Fortress and Cathedral
Institute of Russian Literature
Rostral Columns
Zoological Museum
Smolny Institute

5
The Strelka
Naval Musuem
Winter Palace
Field of Mars
Mikhailovsky Palace
Bolshoi Drama Theater
THE ADMIRALTY SIDE

6
Vasilyevsky Island
The Kunstkammer
The Hermitage
Russian Museum
Theater of Comedies and Tragedies
The Admiralty
Alexander Column and Palace Square
Anichkov Bridge

7
Senate Square and The Bronze Horseman
St. Isaac's Cathedral
Gostiny Dvor
Fontanka Canal
Maly Theater
Nevsky Prospekt
Alexander Nevsky Square
Neva River

8
Maryinsky Theater
Neva River

The Admiralty	E6	Bolshoi Drama Theater	H6	Gulf of Finland	L,M 1,2,3
The Admiralty Side	D-J 4-8	*The Bronze Horseman*	E6	The Hermitage	F5
Alexander Column	F6	Field of Mars	G5	Institute of Russian Literature	E5
Alexander Nevsky Square	J8	Finland Railway Station	H3	Kirov Stadium	A2
Anichkov Bridge	G,H 6	Fontanka Canal	F,G 6,7,8	The Kunstkammer	E5
Artillery Museum	F4	Gostiny Dvor	G 6,7	Lake Ladoga	O1

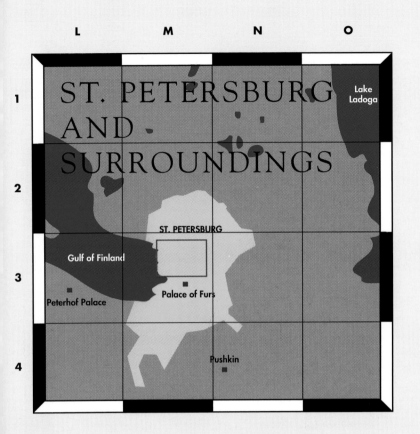

St. Petersburg and Surroundings

GLOSSARY

canal: An artificial waterway used for boat traffic

caulk: To fill cracks in order to prevent leaks

Communism: System in which most capital and property belong to the state rather than to individuals and private corporations

conspirator: Person who secretly schemes with others

delta: Land at the mouth of a river, formed by silt that washes downstream

frigate: Warship powered by sails

icon: In the Eastern Orthodox church, a religious image painted on a wooden panel

imposing: Large, impressive, almost frightening

labyrinth: Maze

ordeal: Challenge involving great hardship

orthodox: Following a strict set of rules or teachings

peasant: Poor farmer, usually one who works land owned by someone else

plunder: To steal openly, as an invading enemy during a war

serf: A virtual slave working on the estate of a wealthy landowner

thoroughfare: A broad avenue

tributary: Stream that feeds into a river

tsar: Emperor of Russia

Picture Identifications

Cover: Catherine Palace, members of a folk troupe, stacking doll
Page 1: Russian girls
Pages 4-5: Hermitage Museum
Pages 8-9: Group of Russian girls playing in a fountain at Peterhof Palace
Pages 20-21: *Peter the Great at Deptford Dock*, a painting of the tsar as he began his journey to western Europe in 1698
Pages 34-35: "Waltz of the Flowers," a scene from *The Nutcracker* ballet
Pages 44-45: St. Nicholas Cathedral

Photo Credits ©:

Wolfgang Kaehler — cover (background), 6 (right), 11
New England Stock Photo — Frank Siteman, cover (left), 19; Jeff Greenberg, 12 (right)
Comstock — cover (right), 43 (right), 47 (bottom), 52 (top), 53 (left); Adam Tanner, 51 (top)
Monkmeyer/Rashid — 1
KK&A, Ltd. — 3, 10 (bottom left), 13, 14-15, 25 (top), 26 (top), 33 (left), 36 (top), 38-39 (bottom), 40 (left), 47 (top), 60, 61
Folio, Inc. — Patricia Lanza, 4-5
Photri, Inc. — 6 (left), 7, 18 (bottom), 33 (right), 42, 44-45, 46, 56 (left), 57 (left)
Photo Edit — Bonnie Kamin, 8-9
Tony Stone Images, Inc. — Sylvain Grandadam, 10 (top), 49 (left); Vince Streano, 23; David Hanson, 25 (bottom); Paul Harris, 36 (bottom right); Christopher Arnesen, 50; Ed Pritchard, 55
Steve Raymer — 10 (bottom right), 18 (top), 36 (bottom left), 40 (right), 41, 48, 59
H. Armstrong Roberts — J. Greenberg/Camerique, 12 (left); B. Krubner, 56 (right)
Liaison International — Ed Lallo, 14 (left), 38 (top), 52 (bottom); Lyn Hughes, 37; Wolfgang Kaehler, 49 (right)
Unicorn Stock Photos — Jeff Greenberg, 15 (top), 17 (top), 32, 51 (bottom), 53 (right)
Bonnie Kamin — 16 (left)
Root Resources — Mary & Lloyd McCarthy, 16-17 (bottom), 54
AKG Photo, London — 20-21, 22 (left), 27, 28, 29, 30, 31
Stock Montage, Inc. — 22 (right)
Impact Visuals — Richard R. Renaldi, 24, 39 (top)
Corbis-Bettmann — 26 (bottom)
Migdoll — 34-35
Carl Purcell — 43 (left)
Ric Ergenbright Photography — Robert Ivy, 57 (top right)
Michele Burgess — 57 (bottom right)

INDEX

Page numbers in boldface type indicate illustrations

TO FIND OUT MORE

BOOKS

Buettner, Dan. *Sovietrek: A Journey by Bicycle across Russia.* Minneapolis: Lerner, 1992.

Carrión, Esther. *The Empire of the Czars.* The World Heritage series. Chicago: Childrens Press, 1994.

Geography Department, Lerner Publications. *Russia, Then and Now.* Minneapolis: Lerner, 1992.

Gilies, John. *The New Russia.* Discovering Our Heritage series. Parsipany, N.J.: Silver Burdett, 1994.

Hanmer, Trudy. *Leningrad—Siege, 1941-1944.* New York: Macmillan, 1992.

Jacobsen, Karen. *The Russian Federation.* New True Books series. Chicago: Childrens Press, 1994.

Kort, Michael. *Russia.* New York: Facts on File, 1995.

Kotlyarskaya, Elena. *Women in Society: Russia.* Tarrytown, N.Y.: Marshall Cavendish, 1994.

Resnick, Abraham. *The Commomwealth of Independent States.* Enchantment of the World series. Chicago: Childrens Press, 1993.

Stein, R. Conrad. *The Siege of Leningrad.* World at War series. Chicago: Childrens Press, 1983.

Torchinsky, Oleg. *Russia.* Cultures of the World series. Tarrytown, N.Y.: Marshall Cavendish, 1994.

ONLINE SITES

A Brief Visit to Russia
http://www.hyperion.com/~koreth/russia/
A travelogue of one man's visit to Russia, with stories, pictures, maps, and links, including St. Petersburg and Moscow.

Alexander Palace Time Machine
http://www.travelogix.com/emp/batchison/
Visit the home of Nicholas II, the last tsar of Russia. Explore the rooms, see how the children lived, and see wondrous palace treasures. Plus history, a map of the village, cathedrals, the Faberge collection and other works of art, and much more!

Destination St. Petersburg
http://www.lonelyplanet.com.au/dest/eur/stp.htm
Find out how St. Petersburg was built on swamps, take a tour of the city's museums, cathedrals, palaces, and fortresses, and see a slide show.

Exploring St. Petersburg
http://www.interknowledge.com/russia/peter01.htm
More historical sites, theaters, and cathedrals, plus a calendar of events, the 4-day weather forecast, and stunning photos.

The Fresh Guide to St. Petersburg
http://www.online.ru/sp/fresh/
Find out what it's really like to live in St. Petersburg. Learn about the city's history, culture, and "tourist things" from a different perspective. Also, get some help with the Russian language.

The Hermitage and the Winter Palace
http://www.interknowledge.com/russia/peter02.htm
Visit one of the world's largest museums, with more than 3 million works of art on display! Then drop in on the residence of the tsars.

Portrait of St. Petersburg
http://www.cs.utah.edu/~efros/spb.html
A photo tour of some of the city's best views, including St. Isaac's Cathedral, the canals, and St. Petersburg University.

St. Petersburg, Russia
http://www.city.net/countries/russia/st_petersburg/
News, weather, maps, city information, travel tips, and links to other sites.

The St. Petersburg Times
http://www.spb.su/times/
Read the current and past issues of one of the city's largest newspapers.

ABOUT THE AUTHOR

Deborah Kent grew up in Little Falls, New Jersey, and received a B.A. in English from Oberlin College. She earned a master's degree from Smith College School for Social Work. After working for four years at the University Settlement House in New York City, she moved to San Miguel de Allende in central Mexico. There she wrote her first young-adult novel, *Belonging*.